ENGLISH GLASS

W. B. HONEY

*WITH
8 PLATES IN COLOUR
AND
26 ILLUSTRATIONS IN
BLACK & WHITE*

COLLINS · 14 ST. JAMES'S PLACE · LONDON
MCMXLVI

PRODUCED BY
ADPRINT LIMITED LONDON

PRINTED IN GREAT BRITAIN BY
THE SUN ENGRAVING CO LTD LONDON AND WATFORD
ON MELLOTEX BOOK PAPER MADE
BY TULLIS RUSSELL AND CO LTD MARKINCH SCOTLAND

LIST OF ILLUSTRATIONS

PLATES IN COLOUR

NAILSEA JUG
Late eighteenth or early nineteenth century

BRISTOL WHITE-GLASS ENAMEL-PAINTED VASE
Mid-eighteenth century

WINEGLASS PAINTED BY WILLIAM BEILBY
Mid-eighteenth century

COUNTRY-MARKET JUGS
Late eighteenth or early nineteenth century

NAILSEA JUG AND FLASKS
Late eighteenth and first half of the nineteenth century

EARLY-VICTORIAN GLASS FOUNTAIN WITH BIRDS

GLASS VASE AND BOWL DESIGNED BY KEITH MURRAY
Stevens & Williams, Limited, Brierly Hill, Stourbridge

LARGE GLASS VASE
James Powell & Sons, Limited, Whitefriars Glassworks, Wealdstone

BLACK AND WHITE ILLUSTRATIONS

PAGE

GLASS-MAKER'S CHAIR 5
Woodcut from Apsley Pellatt's *Curiosities of Glass-making*, 1849

INTERIOR OF A GLASS-HOUSE 7
Woodcut from Apsley Pellatt's *Curiosities of Glass-making*, 1849

GLASS-MAKER'S TOOLS 11
Engraving from Haudicquer de Blancourt's *The Art of Glass*, 1699

TUDOR MEDICINE-BOTTLES 13

THE CHESTERFIELD "FLUTE-GLASS," *c.*1663 15
Sir Richard Garton Collection

VERZELINI GLASS, 1583 18
Hamilton Clements Collection

RAVENSCROFT EWER, *c.* 1675 21
Cecil Higgins Collection

BOWL AND COVER IN BAROQUE STYLE 22
Late seventeenth century
Formerly in the Joseph Bles Collection

BALUSTER WINE-GLASS 23
Early eighteenth century

GROUP OF GLASSES 24
Early eighteenth century

GROUP OF GLASSES 25
Second quarter of the eighteenth century

GROUP OF CUT GLASS 27
Middle and late eighteenth century

BRISTOL BLUE-GLASS BOX 28
Third quarter of the eighteenth century

PAGE

BRISTOL BODKIN-CASE AND SCENT-BOTTLE 29
Third quarter of the eighteenth century

BRISTOL SCENT-BOTTLES 31
Second half of the eighteenth century

GROUP OF ENGRAVED GLASSES 34
Middle of the eighteenth century

GROUP OF CUT GLASSES 35
Late eighteenth and early nineteenth centuries

VASE 37
Late eighteenth century
Formerly in the Joseph Bles Collection

DECANTER-BOTTLE 38
With medallion stamped : *T. Ridge* 1720

MODERN CARBOY 39
Green bottle-glass

VASE DESIGNED BY CLYNE FARQUHARSON 43
John Walsh Walsh, Limited, Birmingham

DECANTER AND GLASSES 44
James Powell & Sons, Limited, Whitefriars Glassworks, Wealdstone

DECANTER AND GLASSES 45
Thomas Webb & Corbett, Limited, Stourbridge

BOWL DESIGNED BY BARNABY POWELL 46
James Powell & Sons, Limited, Whitefriars Glassworks, Wealdstone

DISH DESIGNED AND MADE BY TOM HILL 47
James Powell & Sons, Limited, Whitefriars Glassworks, Wealdstone

OVEN-GLASS CASSEROLE 48
Phoenix Glassware Co., Birmingham

INTERIOR OF A GLASS-HOUSE
Woodcut from Apsley Pellatt's *Curiosities of Glass-making*, 1849

INTRODUCTION:

THE ORIGIN AND NATURE OF GLASS

GLASS is nowadays so familiar that many people take it for granted, without ever considering how it is made, or what part it has played in the history of human customs or as the medium of a branch of creative art. Yet, next to pottery, it ranks as chief among the "arts of fire," and even more than pottery stands for the miraculous transformation of common materials by the action of fire into something wonderful. Mere sand and ashes become a brilliant crystalline substance capable of a thousand delightful uses.

Glass may, in fact, be regarded as an artificial form of the mineral known as rock crystal. Not only is it closely akin in chemical composition, but the appearance of crystal has commonly been the ideal of the maker of glass, who has more than once in its history borrowed the name for his productions. Moreover the names of glass and crystal, and the comparison with ice which both words suggest, are appropriate in a less obvious way; the shaping of glass depends on its fluidity and plasticity when hot, making it subject to the will of the craftsman, whose rhythmical movements are recorded, as it were frozen, in its cooled form. Glass has, of course, its own special order of beauty in colour and in the play of light within its substance; and other ideals than a

7

clear brilliance have sometimes been sought, with beautiful results. But a "water-white" crystal clearness has been the quality most often sought by the glass-maker, and no glass has reached this ideal with greater success than the English-invented "glass-of-lead," sometimes known as "lead crystal."

The origin of glass lies so far back in the pre-history of the Eastern Mediterranean that scholars are still unable to say how and where and precisely when it was first made. As a material for objects of use and ornament it was not suddenly invented in the form in which we now know it. It was a gradual discovery and for at least two thousand years was used in the making of decorative small objects, before the invention of the blowing-tube brought the now-familiar forms of useful glassware.

The story of the invention of glass in Syria as told by Pliny is not now accepted, and it seems probable that the earliest material of the character of glass was first used not alone but in the form of a blue glaze with which in pre-dynastic Egypt, perhaps as early as 4000 B.C., beads of stone were coated. Such a blue glaze, coloured with a copper compound, was probably discovered by accident and used to fabricate beads in imitation of turquoise and other greatly prized blue and green stones. The earliest glass vessels, again Egyptian and dating from about the 15th century B.C., were made by an adaptation of this bead-covering technique; threads of hot ductile glass were wound upon a core of clay and sand which was afterwards removed. Small vessels and decorative objects continued to be made by this process and by moulding and modelling, until just before the beginning of the Christian era, when a revolutionary change in practice was brought about by the invention, apparently in Syria, of the glass-blowing-tube. No technical change of comparable importance took place thenceforward until the introduction in the 19th century of machinery for bottle-making and the "pressing" of glass in moulds, and the large-scale manufacture of glass in sheets.

THE TECHNIQUE OF GLASS-MAKING

GLASS is essentially an artificial compound produced by the fusion of silica in the form of sand, flint or quartz, with the aid of an alkaline flux, normally either potash, or soda. These are the essential ingredients, but to make a tough and durable glass small quantities of other substances, such as lime or one of the oxides of lead, are in practice required. Quartz and rock crystal, which the glassmakers have so often striven to imitate, are themselves almost pure silica. Pure silica may in fact be melted to form a glass, but the very high temperature required rules this out for all but small laboratory vessels required to resist great heat. The soda alkali was in the past usually obtained from the ash of certain marine plants, while the potash was produced by burning bracken or beechwood. At the present day the potash is prepared from saltpetre and from the commercial potassium

NAILSEA JUG
Late eighteenth or early nineteenth century

BRISTOL WHITE-GLASS ENAMEL-PAINTED VASE
Mid-eighteenth century

carbonate known as "pearl ash," while the soda is made from common salt. Lime was added in various forms, such as chalk or limestone. An oxide of lead was used as an ingredient from early times, especially in coloured glass, whose brilliance it enhanced; lead also facilitated the working of glass by increasing its fusibility. Lead glass was in fact specifically mentioned in a text of the 12th century as the material of imitation gems. But a workable glass containing lead in considerable quantity and capable of being formed into vessels was not made before about 1675, when the experiments of Ravenscroft produced the English lead glass, whose remarkable qualities will be described in due course. In both "paste" gems and the English "glass metal" (as it is called), glass-of-lead is distinguished by its brilliancy.

Glass is naturally seldom free from colour. The common presence of traces of iron as an impurity in sand usually gives it a greenish tone, and to obtain a crystal "whiteness" use is made of a decolourising agent in the form of an oxide of manganese, once known as "glass-maker's soap." "Common" or bottle-glass was not so treated.

Deliberate colouring is produced by the addition of metallic oxides such as iron for green, copper for turquoise blue or green, cobalt for blue, and manganese for amethyst pink or purple. All these have been in use for a very long time. The ruby-red of medieval stained glass was also obtained from copper, but another ruby red and a pink, from gold, were 17th-century discoveries. A silver compound to give a yellow surface-stain had been for long employed by the makers of medieval and later window glass, when fresh use was made of it in the 19th century. A dense opaque milk white was given by an oxide of tin; this was used also in the glaze or "enamel" of maiolica and delftware and other sorts of pottery, whence it is sometimes misleadingly called "enamel glass"; semi-opaque and opalescent "milk-and-water" glass was produced by an arsenic compound or by the use of calcined bones. Modern chemistry has added new colours too numerous to mention here.

These ingredients have generally been in practice mixed with a proportion of old broken glass (called "cullet"), partly to help the fusing, but also for the sake of economy, since the waste from the glass-factory itself could be utilised in this way, while at certain periods in England, on account of Excise Duties, it was possible to buy broken glass at a cost much less than that of the ingredients required to make it afresh.

For the melting together of the ingredients a dome-shaped fire-clay pot or crucible two or three feet high was for long the normal container. The making by hand, drying and firing of these pots was a highly skilled operation. They were ranged above a furnace heated by wood or coal. In early times vast quantities of wood fuel were consumed by the glass-makers, who were compelled to move from place to place in the forests as their supplies gave out. English glass-makers were the first to employ pit-coal, in the early part of the 17th century, and its use soon spread to other countries. Oil, gas and electricity have frequently been employed since the 19th century.

In a glass-house run on traditional lines using hand labour, such as that of Messrs. James Powell & Sons, formerly of Whitefriars in London and now of Wealdstone, Middlesex, the glass-pots are arranged in a ring round the furnace. Through an opening in the shoulder the molten glass is taken up by the workman. When melted, glass is more or less fluid, and very sticky, adhering to an iron tube or rod thrust into it. It is also very ductile, and may be drawn out, without breaking, into threads of great length. When a lump of molten glass has been "gathered" at the end of the iron tube and shaped into a globular or cylindrical mass by rolling on an iron table (called a "marver"), it may be blown into a bubble, and to this property was due the revolutionary change of practice already referred to. The bubble may be elongated by swinging, pressed or rolled, cut with shears and otherwise manipulated or transferred to an iron rod (called a "pontil" or "puntee") for inversion and further working. The plasticity of the glass during the shaping is maintained by repeated re-heating in the mouth of the furnace, which also restores the brilliant fused surface-condition known as fire polish. By constant rotation of the tube or rod the shapes are kept symmetrical about a central line like a pot thrown on the wheel or a piece of turnery. The working of glass by these hand processes, which call for great dexterity and a peculiar gift of rhythmical movement, has changed but little since Roman times. The same simple tools, and above all the chair in which the principal workman sits, with long flat parallel arms on which the rod is rotated by rolling, have continued in use until the present day.

The glass bubble can also be blown into a mould of baked clay, stone or metal. This process, which was perhaps the earliest of all forms of blowing, eventually led to the application of machine power to glass-manufacture. Complicated apparatus for mechanically blowing bottles in metal moulds was perfected in America towards the end of the 19th century, and the process has been extended to the making of other sorts of vessel of bottle type, such as electric-light bulbs. As many as fifteen thousand bottles a day may be turned out by one of the larger machines. Some modern bottle-making machinery makes use of "pressing" as well as of mechanical blowing.

In the "pressing" of glass, another 19th-century invention, comparable with the "jolleying" of the potter, a quantity of molten glass is placed in a mould giving the outside shape of the vessel, and a plunger is thrust into it to give the inside shape, forcing the glass upwards and outwards to fill the mould. Pressing was used at first as a means of imitating cut glass, but can equally well be applied to the mass-production of well-designed modern shapes.

All manufactured glass, whether made by hand or by machinery, requires to be toughened by annealing, a process by which it is placed in a heated chamber (called a "*lehr*" or "leer") and gradually cooled. This removes internal strains and stresses produced by its shaping and uneven cooling, which otherwise would leave it brittle and unserviceable. The behaviour of the glass toys known as "Prince Rupert's drops" is a demonstration of the

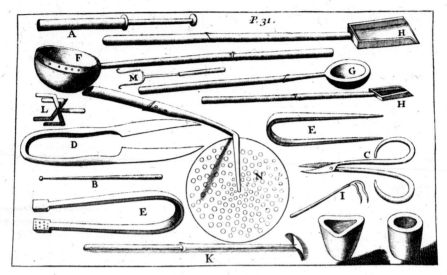

GLASS-MAKER'S TOOLS
Engraving from Haudicquer de Blancourt's *The Art of Glass*, 1699

properties of glass that has not been annealed. They are pear-shaped beads with a "tail," made by dropping molten glass into water, and their internal state of strain is such that they collapse into powder when the tail is broken off.

The most characteristic sorts of glass decoration are those which exploit its peculiar plasticity and ductility when hot. The rhythmical shaping of handles, the drawing out and tooling of stems into wings and discs and "knops" (or swellings), the waving of mouths and feet, and the application of threads tooled or melted in, are such types of decoration. Differing composition and consistency in the molten glass may suggest variety of treatment; one sort (such as the Venetian) may be fluid and encourage rapid elaborate manipulation, while others (such as the English lead-glass) are stiffer and call for more simple treatment.

Other types of decoration are shared with other materials. Thus the engraving and cutting of glass on the lapidary's wheel are grinding processes used originally on crystal and other stones. The wheel consists of an iron or copper disc, large or small, fed with emery and water, on to which the glass surface to be engraved is pressed. The engraving of glass has been condemned by (amongst others) John Ruskin, on the ground that it "conceals its ductility and confuses it with crystal"; but these critics have overlooked the special light-transmitting qualities of different sorts of glass. On the other hand painting in vitreous fusible enamels fired in a muffle-kiln is a process shared with porcelain and indeed has often been adopted in conscious rivalry with it.

Peculiar to glass, though suggested by such stones as layered onyx, is the process of "flashing" or "casing" it with another colour by dipping the gathering before blowing it, the coating being afterwards partially cut through to leave a pattern of contrasting colours. A similar result may be produced by cutting through a surface stained "silver yellow" by the process already mentioned as familiar in window-glass-making.

Scratching the surface with a diamond-point is a mode of decoration of great antiquity, while etching it with hydrofluoric acid and roughening it in patterns with a blast of sand or iron dust are relatively modern processes, especially well adapted to mechanised large-scale industry.

These, then, are the chief processes used in the making and decorating of English glass vessels, such as are generally meant when "glass" is referred to. The English word, however, covers the meanings of three French words —*verrerie* (vessels or glassware in general), *vitrail* (window glass), and *verroterie* (glass beads, jewellery, etc.). The last two of these lie outside the scope of this small book, but may be mentioned briefly here.

Small window panes were made by the Roman glass-workers apparently by "casting," or pouring the molten "metal" on to a flat surface. But larger pieces were made in medieval times and later by two adaptations of the blowing-process. By what was called the "crown" or "Normandy" process a bubble was opened while still on the rod. This, rapidly rotated, caused the bubble (continually reheated in the mouth of the furnace) to spread by centrifugal force into a nearly flat disc as much as four feet in diameter, with a thick boss or "bull's eye" in the middle. From this disc flat diamond-shaped or rectangular pieces were cut. By the "broad" or "Lorraine" process the ends were cut off an elongated bubble, and the resulting cylinder was cut longitudinally with shears and opened out and flattened. "Crown" glass shows a slight concavity and a faint rippling in concentric circles; in "broad" glass the ripples are straight.

Machinery was in the 19th century applied to the cylinder-process. An iron ring dipped into a tank of molten glass was drawn upwards to form a cylinder as much as fifty feet high; this was afterwards opened and flattened. Sheets up to six feet in width and of almost unlimited length are also produced by drawing out the glass on an iron bar dipped along its length in the molten "metal"; the sheet so produced is then passed between rollers, cooling as it proceeds. "Plate glass" was originally made by pouring ("casting") the molten "metal" on to an iron table where it was rolled and finally ground and polished with abrasives to a perfectly flat surface on both sides. Modern machinery enables polished plate to be made by passing the sheet between rollers, producing flatter surfaces requiring less grinding.

Glass jewellery (*verroterie*) is generally made of an easily fusible lead glass, capable of being worked with simple tools in the heat of a lamp. Glass rods and tubes are thus fashioned by hand into toy figures, flowers and other decorative small objects.

TUDOR MEDICINE-BOTTLES

ROMAN AND MEDIEVAL GLASS
IN ENGLAND

WHEN Britain became part of the Roman Empire much glass was imported into the country, not only from Egypt and from Syria, where a great industry had grown up with the invention of glass-blowing, but also from the neighbouring province of Gaul. There Syrian emigrants had started numerous glass-houses which were already flourishing in the 2nd and 3rd centuries. Whether glass was also made in Britain, as well as imported, is still a matter of dispute. Even if it was made here, as seems probable, it could not be described as British glass; it would have followed the fashions prevailing in other parts of the Roman Empire. Nevertheless the tradition of Roman glass was the inevitable inspiration of many sorts of English, as of most other later European glass. Within two or three centuries after the invention of glass-blowing, the artisans of the Roman Empire had mastered almost every glass-technique subsequently in use. It is in fact tempting to say that Roman glass was the best ever made. In command of colour (doubtless inherited from the Egyptians), in the invention of austere and measured Classical forms, as well as of wild fantastic improvisations, and even in the use of engraving and cutting, alike in objects of luxury and articles of use, the Roman glass-maker was supreme.

With the decline of the Empire and the eventual withdrawal of the Romans from Britain, such glass as continued to be made in the North lost its Classical character; but several interesting types, such as some so-called "trunk-

13

beakers" with claw-like appendages and some beautiful elongated cone-shaped cups, survive to represent the period of the Invasions and Migrations and the "Anglo-Saxon" period in England. There is no proof, however, or even probability, that any of these "Frankish" or "Teutonic" glasses were made in England, though many have been found here. By the 7th and 8th centuries, at all events, it would seem that no glass was being made in Britain, since there is a record of Abbots of Wearmouth and Jarrow then asking for glass-makers to be sent to England from Gaul and the Rhineland.

On the Continent the Roman art survived and the Roman tradition is still recognisable in the cups and small bottles roughly made of imperfect greenish metal, which continued to be produced throughout the medieval period. These form a link between Roman glass and the Northern European glass which in the 15th century came to vigorous life again and produced many masterpieces. At the same time, another and much more influential renascence of glass-making was in progress in Italy, particularly at Venice.

The medieval Northern glass is variously known by the German name *Waldglas* (forest glass), having been made in the forests, the ash of the beech-wood used for firing serving as the source of potash alkali, and as *verre de fougère* in France, from the use of bracken ash for the same purpose. It was never colourless, but had a greenish tinge from the presence of iron in the sand used; and the fully developed Northern glass-metal of the 15th century and later was of a most attractive sea-green colour, no doubt produced deliberately. The *Waldglas* was made at many places in France, Belgium and Germany.

How soon emigrants took the craft to England cannot be stated with certainty, but records make it clear that already in the 13th century, glass-makers from Normandy were settled in what was then the forest region of the Weald of Kent, Surrey and Sussex. They were chiefly makers by the "crown" process of coloured window-glass, of which this was, of course, a period of the highest achievement. By the 16th century glass-makers from Lorraine had begun to compete with the Normans in the Weald. All used great quantities of wood as fuel, moving from place to place as their supplies were exhausted. In this use of wood they were rivals of the important Sussex iron-founders, and eventually some of the Lorraine families as well as some of the Normans, moved to Hampshire (Buckholt), and on to Gloucestershire (Newent, Forest of Dean, Woodchester) and to North Staffordshire (Bishop's Wood, Blore Park). Members of the same Lorraine families of Ensell (Hennezel) and Tyzack (Thisac) are recorded from the early part of the 17th century onwards at Old Swinford and elsewhere in the Stourbridge area, which was to become and still is one of the most important glass-making regions in England. These men from Lorraine were again chiefly makers of window-glass, using the "broad" process, but made vessels in *Waldglas* also. These are known from fragments found in excavations on the sites of glass-houses, and included many small phials or medicine-bottles of tapering conical or cylindrical form. Beaker-shaped drinking-glasses, often ribbed and standing on a spreading foot, are also found, as well as stemmed goblets already showing the Venetian influence which was soon to be paramount. The degree to which the Roman tradition was maintained in these vessels is shown by the fact that they are often mistaken for Roman work and have frequently been exhibited as such in English provincial museums.

GLASS
MADE IN ENGLAND
IN THE VENETIAN STYLE

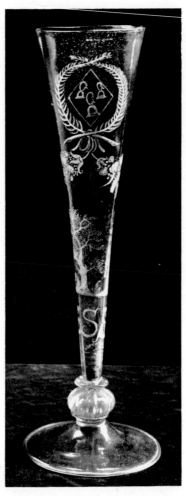

THE rise of the Venetian industry dates from the 15th century, when the making of an almost colourless glass, called "*cristallo*" after the natural stone, brought a new fame to its productions, which had previously been limited to beads and common glass in the medieval styles. Venice (or more accurately Murano) glass thenceforward set the European fashion among the well-to-do for nearly two hundred years. In every country of Europe Venetian glass stood for the new Renaissance styles, as against the medieval or Gothic taste; the latter, however, survived in a modified form, in Germany and elsewhere, as late as the 17th century. Much glass was exported from Venice, but more was made by emigrant Italian workmen who settled in other countries far and wide. Everywhere, with the spread of luxury, glass, and not only Venice glass, became fashionable. For England an Elizabethan writing in 1586 testified to the preference given to glass over even silver and gold, telling how "our gentilitie as lothing those mettals (because of the plentie) do now generallie choose rather the Venice glasses . . . such is the nature of man . . . that it most coveteth things difficult to be atteyned . . . and as this is seen in the gentilitie, so in the wealthie communaltie the like desire of glasse is not neglected . . .

THE CHESTERFIELD "FLUTE-GLASS"
c. 1663

15

the poorest also will have glasse if they may; but sith the Venician is somewhat too deare for them, they content themselves with such as are made at home of ferne and burned stone." (This was, of course, the period of the Spanish-American silver and the raiding of the galleons.)

Emigrant Venetian glass-workers reached England at least as early as 1549, but most of them, temperamental as Italians and glass-blowers commonly are, did not stay. In 1570, however, more Italians were engaged to work at a glass-house in Crutched Friars in London, and from this time onwards for more than a century glass in Venetian style continued to be made in England. In 1575, after the Crutched Friars house had been burnt down, the first considerable figure in the history of glass-making in England, the Venetian Jacopo Verzelini (or Jacob Versaline, as he came to be called, b. 1523, d. 1606), obtained from Queen Elizabeth a privilege for twenty-one years to make Venice glasses in London and teach the craft to Englishmen. His glass-house was in Broad Street, in the city of London.

In 1592, Verzelini's privilege was taken over by Sir Jerome Bowes, who was a company-promoter and not a practical glass-maker at all, and for many years after this the industry in England was controlled by profit-seeking would-be monopolists importing Venice glass and employing Italians, until eventually, after the Restoration (in 1673 to be precise), the London Glass-Sellers' Company took up the matter and were instrumental in creating an independent art of English glass. The outstanding figure in the period of the monopolists was Sir Robert Mansell, a retired admiral, who by 1618 had bought out all his rivals; and the most noteworthy technical change was the use towards 1610–1615 of pit coal as fuel in place of wood.

The identification of the glass made in the various European countries à la façon de Venise, as it is often called, has always been difficult, and of the great number of 16th- and 17th-century specimens attributed to Venice many still unidentified must have been made abroad. The glasses of the kind made in England are no exception, and the matter is complicated by the fact that the Italians generally reached this country by way of the Netherlands, where Antwerp was the most active centre of Italian glassmaking outside Italy. The glasses made in England would thus tend to form a subdivision of the Netherlands class of Venetian-style glasses. Excavations made in 1874 on the site of Verzelini's Broad Street glass-house produced inconclusive results. Unlike broken pottery and kiln wasters, broken and defective glasses have intrinsic value as cullet for remelting, and are seldom as abundant on a glass-house site as the sherds found where a pottery has been.

The shapes of the glasses are, moreover, no certain guide, since it is known that specific orders were sent to Venice, and some drawings actually survive, with the instructions sent to the glass-maker Morelli by a London firm of glass-sellers, John Greene and Michael Measey, between 1666 and 1673. These, of course, come late in the period here in question, but they are evidence of the custom prevailing.

16

WINEGLASS PAINTED BY WILLIAM BEILBY
Mid-eighteenth century

COUNTRY-MARKET JUGS

Late eighteenth or early nineteenth century

Certain rare glasses in Venetian style, dated and inscribed with English names and mottoes, have for long been the only work positively ascribed to Verzelini. They are wide goblets with hollow knopped stems, and are mostly engraved with the diamond point. The earliest recorded is dated 1577. One such glass bears the name of John and "Jone" "Dier" (1581). Two others (1583 and 1586) bear the motto of the Pewterers' Company of London—"In God is all my trust." With the engraving on these surviving glasses, the antiquary Albert Hartshorne with considerable probability associated the recorded name of one Anthony de Lysle, an engraver of pewter, who came from France, where he presumably engraved another goblet, now in the Musée de Cluny, Paris, of precisely the same character as in those with English inscriptions; this bears a decoration of *fleur-de-lys* and the date 1578. Very closely similar in style of engraving is a cylindrical glass of German form in the Victoria and Albert Museum, inscribed with the name of William Smith (b. 1530, d. 1618), together with his arms and those of his wife Veronica Altensteig of Nuremberg, where he was living in 1582, the date on the glass. It seems probable therefore that the glasses engraved by this wandering artist were of various origins.

With these so-called Verzelini glasses are associated another, of the usual form but purple in colour, and another dated 1590 and bearing the gilt (not engraved) arms of the Vintners' Company of London and the name "Wenijfrid Geares."

Apart from these rare inscribed specimens, the productions of Verzelini and his Italian successors are probably to be found among the many glasses with hollow stems, either with moulded or gadrooned knops or of elongated baluster form. The former include a glass in the Victoria and Albert Museum dated 1602, diamond-engraved in the de Lysle manner, bearing the name of Barbara Potter. Of the latter type, which shows a kinship in the form of stem with the silver cups of Charles I's reign, fragments have been found in London excavations, and many complete specimens survive in this country.

The middle part of the 17th century, the period of the monopolists, is poorly represented by actual glasses to be claimed as made in England. Mansell employed a succession of Italians, one of whom, Paolo Mazzola, was recorded elsewhere as a maker of *verres ornés*. These were presumably winged or "serpent-glasses" of a well-known type; the stem of such a glass appears in fact to have been found in the Broad Street excavations. The more extravagant of these, however, are probably Netherlandish work, though certain light-winged glasses, not uncommon in this country, were perhaps made here.

For the third quarter of the 17th century a confusion with the Netherlandish glass is more than ever likely. A tall "flute glass" of a favourite Dutch form, once in the possession of an Earl of Chesterfield, bears diamond-engravings of the Royal Arms of England, together with those of Scudamore and the date 1663, and has on that account been confidently classed as English work. A similar "flute" in the Royal Albert Memorial Museum, Exeter, is

VERZELINI GLASS, 1583
Hamilton Clements Collection

18

engraved with a portrait bust of Charles II, and the inscription "God bless King Charles the Second." But this glass is precisely similar in shape and style of engraving to another, in the Wilfred Buckley Collection at the Victoria and Albert Museum, with a portrait of the young William of Orange and the inscription "Vive le Prince." It is at least possible that all these flute glasses were made and decorated in Holland. It has been argued that political relations between England and Holland at that time were unfavourable for this. In precisely this period, however, there is record of a Dutch dealer in London who may well have acted as intermediary.

Another famous glass with a long English tradition is a large straight-sided goblet formerly in the Joseph Bles Collection. This bears a portrait of Charles within a wreath of oak leaves on a formal tree inscribed "Royal Oak" (in memory of the Battle of Worcester when Charles hid in an oak tree), flanked by portraits of the same King and of Catherine of Braganza; it bears also on the back the Royal Arms of England and the date 1663. But this, with its cylindrical bowl and hollow knop, closely resembles another goblet in the Wilfred Buckley Collection, diamond-engraved with a figure-subject and an inscription in Dutch; and like the "Chesterfield flute" and its kindred this "Royal Oak Goblet" seems unlikely to have been made or even decorated in England.

THE CLASSICS
OF ENGLISH GLASS

THE revolution in English glass-making that came in the last quarter of the 17th century was part of a general movement in northern Europe inspired by a determination to be independent of the difficult Italians. In England, too, the Restoration brought a new spirit of scientific enquiry, of which one of the first results was the foundation in 1662 of the Royal Society, and in the same year the standard Italian book on glass-making—the *Arte Vetraria* of Antonio Neri—was translated into English by Christopher Merret. The desire for independence had also an economic aspect, in a growing demand for national self-sufficiency in industry and trade, parallel with the Mercantilism of Colbert in France.

In 1673 the London Glass-Sellers' Company took the step of engaging a chemist named George Ravenscroft (b. 1618, d. 1681) to undertake glass-researches for them, with the help of an Italian named Da Costa; in that year he was granted a patent for seven years for the invention of "a new sort of crystalline glass resembling rock-crystal." The Company kept up two glass-houses, one at the Savoy in London, the other, used chiefly for experiment, at Henley-on-Thames, and here from 1674 onwards Ravenscroft worked. It was evidently the Company's intention to provide an English substitute for the Venetian *cristallo*, made of English materials only. The early adoption of the term "flint-glass" for Ravenscroft's productions may indicate that a new source of silica had been found in the English flints, replacing the imported Venetian pebbles; for the alkali, potash was substituted for the Venetian soda. The relative infusibility of the flints may have made it necessary to increase the proportion of an unfamiliar alkali, and excess of this brought a fault in the form of "crisselling"—a network or clouding of fine interior cracks. This is a well-known and progressive disease or decay of glass, always due to excess of alkali, leading eventually to complete disintegration. Some other fluxing agent was evidently called for, and this was found in an oxide of lead. Lead had, of course, been used in glass-making long before this, but the lead-glass compositions previously known had been unsuited to the making of vessels. Neri, in his book, had praised it, "as to colour the finest and noblest glass," while his translator and editor Merret added "'tis a thing unpractised in our furnaces, and the reason is because of the exceeding brittleness thereof." But Ravenscroft eventually arrived at a satisfactory composition, and in 1676 it was reported that "the defect in the flint glass (which was formerly observed to crissel and decay)" had been remedied. In the same year it was arranged that the Company's glasses should bear a seal, and Ravenscroft was allowed to use a raven's head as his device for this purpose. From this year, then, 1676, dates the beginning of a truly English art of glass.

Physically the new glass was much heavier, volume for volume, than the Venetian; it was also softer, and fused at a lower temperature. But it was apparently never as fluid as the Venetian, and was less apt for blowing thin and working into elaborate forms. It had an oil-like brilliance and a peculiar darkness in the shadows. More important still, perhaps, in view of its subsequent history, it shared with the earlier lead-glass "paste" a remarkable light-dispersing property, giving it exceptional interior fire. This quality in the English glass, which was naturally more conspicuous in thick-walled vessels and in those cut into facets, approaches that of the diamond, surpassing rock-crystal and all other sorts of glass.

Purple, green and opaque-white glass were also made in forms suggesting that they are of Ravenscroft's period; but they were of little importance compared with his crystal "glass-of-lead."

The new glass satisfied the English taste so well that by the end of the 17th century nearly a hundred glass-houses were making it. Sand was soon substituted for flints, but the name "flint glass" continued, and still continues, to be used for the English lead-glass.

Apart from the glasses with Ravenscroft's own seal and their kindred, and a few others with seals conjecturally attributed to other houses, it is seldom possible to ascribe specimens of old English glass to makers or even places. The customary attributions, based often enough on the unsupported conjectures of an older generation of antiquaries, have far outrun the evidence.

RAVENSCROFT EWER, *c.* 1675
Cecil Higgins Collection

21

BOWL AND COVER IN BAROQUE STYLE
Late seventeenth century

22

There are numerous records of glass-makers, but few surviving glasses to serve as documents for the identification of their productions. Traditional ascriptions are often of very doubtful value. The attribution to Norwich, for example, of certain horizontally ribbed glasses is unsupported by evidence; there is in fact no certain record of a glass-house in that city. Again, the practice of calling almost all milk-white and fine blue glass "Bristol" is also certainly unjustified, as is the contention that all Waterford glass has a blue tinge.

London evidently remained the fashion-leading centre, dictating the forms of wine-glasses and their decoration. At Henley, from 1676 onwards, Ravenscroft was succeeded by one Hawley Bishop, who also took over the Company's Savoy house on Ravenscroft's death in 1681. Other London manufacturers flourished in this period, particularly at Southwark. There continued to be important manufactures at Stourbridge (where the local fireclay was found to be especially valuable for the glass-pots), and at Newcastle-on-Tyne and South Shields in the North, as well as at Bristol and in Ireland.

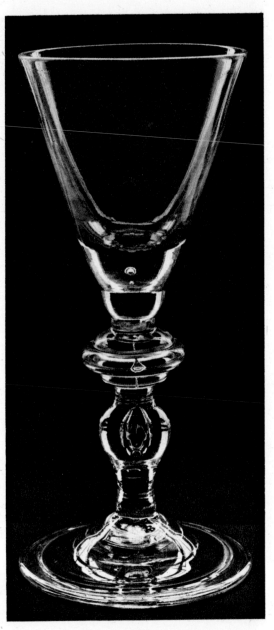

BALUSTER WINE-GLASS
Early eighteenth century

23

GROUP OF GLASSES
Early eighteenth century

The glasses made under Ravenscroft's direction are recognisable by his seal (but less than a dozen of these are known to survive), and by a price-list issued by him in 1677. They range from mugs in forms recalling the Rhenish and Fulham stoneware with which the Glass-Sellers' Company was also concerned, to very large ewers and goblets. Perhaps the most remarkable of all these primitives of English glass are two inverted helmet- or bell-shaped ewers, very boldly ribbed, with massive twisted handles. One of these, now in the Cecil Higgins Collection, bears the seal; the other, in the Wilfred Buckley Collection in the Victoria and Albert Museum, lacks it, but is much crisselled and may be slightly earlier. Some sealed goblets of German *Roemer* form, decorated with raspberry-like impressed pads called "prunts," are perhaps evidence of a desire to break away from Venetian forms; though the *Roemer* was for long the accepted form of glass for Rhenish wine. On the other hand a sealed bowl and certain covered goblets are decorated in a variant of the Venetian style, with lobed "gadrooning" at the base, and extravagant loops, wings and finials. This was doubtless the "extraordinary work" mentioned in Ravenscroft's list. Decoration of "trailed" threads pincered into a network is presumably the decoration described by him as "nipt diamond waies." There are specimens of the sort in the Victoria and Albert

GROUP OF GLASSES
Second quarter of the eighteenth century

Museum with stems enclosing coins (as was frequently the custom from this
time onwards) of 1680 and 1684; but such work continued to be done on
occasion until well into the following century. The Master's chair of the
Glass-sellers' Company, made in 1704, is in fact carved on the back with a
representation of two vessels of the kind.

The style of these primitives is a curious hybrid, a product of the expiring
Venetian fashions and the new English glass. It is nevertheless a genuine
expression of the English baroque, with all the flourish characteristic of the
art of Charles II's reign. It is the analogue in glass of the elaborately wrought
furniture and silver of the time.

Before long, simpler and less grandiloquent forms began to prevail, and
the half-century from about 1690 onwards saw what was probably the finest
of all English glass-making. Some of the best work was done less in decorative vases and goblets than in wine-glasses for actual use, a department in
which Greene's designs for Venetian glass (1666–1673), already mentioned,
went some way towards the creation of an English style. Greene's short-
stemmed glasses with "wrought buttons" or moulded knops gave place in
the latter part of the 17th century to still plainer forms with longer stems, at
first hollow but soon made solid, in conformity with the character of the lead

25

metal. The plain forms of the contemporary silver, encouraged by the softer "Britannia standard" which was obligatory from 1697 to 1718, and particularly that of the reign of Queen Anne (1702–1714), may well have influenced the style of the glass. The taste shown was shared by the other arts of the time— by the architecture, silver and furniture of the period of William and Mary, Anne and the first two Georges. In glass as in architecture it was a taste marked by a love of simplicity and fine proportions rather than ornament.

The typical creation of the period was the wine-glass with solid "baluster" stem formed of discs and knops. These stems are of immense variety, showing an admirable judgement in the assembling of the globular, cylindrical, urn-shaped, and true-baluster knops, and in their proportioning to the size and shape of bowl and foot. The baluster stems were sometimes made to enclose a bubble of air, and a decoration of such "beads" was for long popular. A well-placed ribbing of bowls and feet, with gadrooning and reeding ("incising") sometimes twisted spirally, were other favourite forms of simple decoration. The characteristic 17th-century "trailing" and nipping of threads of glass also survived for a long time.

German influence, due to the importation of glasses under the Treaty of Utrecht (1713) and the accession of the Hanoverian George I in the following year, brought a new type of shouldered stem into fashion, side by side with the baluster. This was of West-German origin, but is erroneously known among English collectors as the "Silesian" stem. In its later forms it is often polygonal and twisted spirally, and is sometimes inverted.

The bowls of the wine-glasses were at first straight-sided funnels, their height not less than that of the stems. In the reign of George I bowls tended to develop a waist and "flare" or curve outwards, and the relative height of the stem was gradually increased.

Besides the wine-glasses and goblets, which were sometimes very large, many smaller vessels were made in beautiful forms. There were short-stemmed glasses for strong ale, sweetmeat-glasses with wide shallow bowls on tall stems, and above all many small glasses believed to have been used for jellies, custards and sillabub. These beautiful vessels were of plain, or ribbed, or boldly faceted forms, with single or double handles, and appear to have been generally served on plain glass salvers with baluster or "Silesian" stems to match. All these types remained current throughout the first half of the 18th century and even later.

The glass candlesticks of the period were also of great beauty, with baluster stems showing the same fine taste in the assembling of knops, air-beaded or plain, or "Silesian" or spirally reeded stems, harmoniously composed with domed, ribbed or "terraced" feet. They are often difficult to date—the beaded knops of the baluster style being sometimes found used in conjunction with the "enamel-twist" stems of the following period.

Throughout the baluster period the heavy lead glass was used lavishly; the bases of wine-glasses were made thick and solid, while edges and feet were

26

GROUP OF CUT GLASS
Middle and late eighteenth century

often folded over, giving added strength. The total impression is one of harmony and repose.

The taste of the succeeding period was inclined to prefer lighter glasses and more decoration. To some extent this change was due to the rococo style then making itself felt in the decorative arts, but it was also in part the result of a gradually increased Excise Duty on glass, imposed to help to provide funds for the wars with France. It was levied (1745-46 onwards) by weight of materials used, and for nearly a hundred years the burden of the Excise affected the forms and character of English glass.

BRISTOL BLUE-GLASS BOX
c. 1750–1775

THE ROCOCO PERIOD

AND THE VOGUE OF DECORATION

THE fashion that favoured lighter glasses was partly due to reaction against the rigid symmetry and occasional heaviness of the baroque style. The rococo brought a new lightness into English decoration. At the same time the Excise Duty in effect encouraged the glass-makers to produce wares whose price represented the work expended on their decoration rather than the amount of glass used in making them; and since the duty was levied by weight the proportion of lead also tended to be lessened, and from the middle of the 18th century onwards the oil-like metal of the baluster period was gradually replaced by a somewhat lighter and more "watery" glass material containing much less lead.

The wine-glasses were of relatively few shapes. Some of these, too, strictly speaking belong to the end of the previous period. Some slender baluster forms with air-beaded stems persisted at least until 1765, in glasses made at Newcastle and elsewhere. The waisted thistle-shaped bowl and the ogee and double ogee had first appeared in the reign of George I but still continued to be made. What are called drawn stems also remained popular. These had a long ancestry, going back indeed to Venetian origins. In this type of wine-glass the stem was not made separately and stuck on, but drawn out from the trumpet-shaped bowl in one piece. It enjoyed renewed popularity as a large glass in the first half of the 18th century, but soon succumbed to the general fashion for lightness. It came again in a shorter form in the 1780's and survived into the 19th century in rough tavern glasses. Straight slender cylindrical stems came into fashion with straight-sided bucket-shaped bowls, though knops were sometimes still used, as already mentioned. These appeared as cusped swellings when submitted to the facet-cutting also fashionable in stems of the middle of the century.

It is for its decoration, however, that the mid-18th-century glass is chiefly valued. The principal methods of decorating the finished glass were by cutting and engraving it on the lapidary's wheel, by scratching it with a diamond-point, and by painting it in enamel colours. But first to be described, since it belongs to the making of the glasses themselves, is the extremely popular decoration of the stems by air-, "incised," enamel-, and coloured "twists." The first of these was developed from the air-bubble or "bead" often enclosed in the knops of the baluster and at the base of the bowl of the drawn-stem glasses. It was made by elongating and twisting a gathering of hot glass containing one or more of these air bubbles. Glasses with air-twists were apparently sometimes called "wormed glasses." The "incised twist" or "wrythen stem" was produced by elongating and twisting a moulded gathering. The "enamel" (opaque white) and coloured (green, red, blue, crimson, etc.) twists were manipulated in the same way as the air bubbles to form threads or flat ribbons of spiral form, sometimes intertwined. Rods of white or coloured glass, arranged round a cylindrical mould, were picked up on a lump of molten glass, which after being covered with clear glass by dipping was drawn out into a rod. This was twisted and if necessary combined with other rods by a repetition of the process, which was essentially the same as an ancient Roman and Venetian technique.

Diamond-point engraving (or scratching) is found on English glasses of various dates, some of which have already been described. But the rococo period produced some especially noteworthy examples. The decoration does not in fact belong strictly speaking to glass-making at all; it could be practised after dinner by an amateur, while the finer examples were evidently the work

BRISTOL BODKIN-CASE AND SCENT-BOTTLE, *c.* 1750–1775

29

of professional engravers on pewter and silver. Among the last-mentioned are the occasional inscriptions in beautiful flourished lettering; a fine baluster-stemmed glass in the Wilfred Buckley Collection is an early example, inscribed "God Bless Queen Ann."

But the most famous of all 18th-century English diamond-engraved speci-mens are those bearing the cipher of the Old Pretender ("J.R.8") in mono-gram, with two or three verses of a Jacobite hymn, precursor of the British National Anthem, ending with the word "Amen." They are of hotly disputed date. Most of them are of drawn stem or baluster type, dating from any time between 1720 and 1750, but at least one is an air-twist glass of a type made at Newcastle from about 1745 onwards. Several bear dates between 1716 and 1749, some of which must be commemorative, or else later additions, since the hymn refers to the Young Pretender (as the "Prince of Wales"), who was not born until 1720. References to the birth in 1725 of Prince Henry, second son of the Old Pretender, are not necessarily contemporary with that event, while "the increase of the Royal familie" may not imply, as has been supposed, a date before the death in 1735 of the Pretender's wife, but may refer to the celibacy of Prince Henry, who became a cardinal in 1747. It had thus appeared probable that the glasses were later than had been sup-posed, when the recent discovery of a fragmentary specimen at Dunvegan Castle, Skye, provided unexpected confirmation. This bears a diamond-engraved inscription in the same hand as the hymn, dated 1747 and referring to a recorded associate of Prince Charles Edward. It suggests a date round about 1745–48 for all the "Amen glasses." The use of the Scottish title James VIII has suggested that the engraving was done in Scotland.

The Jacobite glasses are of no particular importance in the history of English glass-making as such, but association with the cult has given them an interest for collectors. They are found with wheel-engraved and facet-cut decoration and with enamelling, as well as with diamond-point work, and examples of these will be mentioned in due course. The cryptic legends and emblems they bear have been the subject of bitter dispute; it is sometimes even uncertain whether they refer to the Jacobite or to the rival Williamite cause. A large glass belonging to Mr. C. M. Fleury, diamond-engraved with St. George and the Dragon (?) and the date 1761, and inscribed "The Glorious Memory," was claimed by a leading Jacobite authority as a "dis-guised Jacobite glass." But this seems unlikely since another large glass engraved by the same hand is dedicated to Oliver Cromwell. These two specimens bear the signature of George Chapman, an engraver of whom nothing further is known; but the sensitive engraving of flowers on these two glasses entitles them to rank as the finest English work in the technique. The lateness of the dates suggests that they were engraved some considerable time after their making—a possibility always to be borne in mind where decorated glasses are concerned. English glasses were also much used abroad, in Hol-land, for engraving on the wheel and for the characteristic Dutch stippled work in diamond-point, and mistaken conclusions may well be drawn on this account also.

The art of cutting and engraving glass was at this time chiefly a German and Bohemian accomplishment, and in those countries had produced some of its finest masterpieces long before the end of the 17th century. But in England there was no sign of its adoption before the beginning of the following century at the earliest. The first record of the appearance of German cut glass in England is of a sale in 1709, when "a great disturbance" was made by "the Glass Sellers of London whereby the auction could not be carried on." When eventually cutting and engraving were accepted as modes of decoration, they showed a distinct style suggesting an origin to some extent apart. English taste was conservative, it is true, but it may well have been affected by an amply justified preference for plain glasses in the beautiful new English metal. At all events little surviving English cut or engraved glass can be ascribed to dates before the fourth decade of the 18th century. Yet in spite of the absence of specimens there is some evidence of earlier work. In 1719 a London glass-seller, John Akerman, was recorded as employing a Bohemian cutter (believed to be one Haedy), and it is thought that certain "scaloped" and "corner'd brim" glasses seen in London by Lady Grisell Baillie in 1722 and 1727 were his productions. Jerom Johnson, another dealer, advertised in 1739 "all manner of cut glass" including "scallop'd Dessert Glasses in the newest fashion." Two explanations suggest themselves for the scarcity of surviving actual specimens. Either the references were chiefly to imported German glass; or, as is more probable, most of the earlier English specimens were destroyed when no longer in the fashion, for use as "cullet." Such destruction was especially liable to happen in the period from 1745 onwards when the cost of the materials for new glass was so greatly increased by the duty.

Most of the surviving early specimens with cut decoration are in fact sweetmeat-glasses ("dessert glasses") of the "corner'd brim" or "scallop'd"

BRISTOL SCENT-BOTTLES
c. 1750–1800

31

type. They show a style of cutting less influenced by German models than by the art of the English "glass-grinder," whose trade it was to grind mirror-plates and bevel and "scallop" their edges into scrolled, wavy, and faceted forms. Shallow slicing and simple faceting were thus the rule on these early cut glasses. The faceting of stems was perhaps imitated from the German, but in effect showed a characteristic and charming English plainness. Cutting throughout the rococo period remained relatively shallow. Triangular, four-sided and crescent-shaped slices, often in groups with notches at the inter-sections, formed pyramids and diamonds in very low relief; bands of broad fluting and above all a pattern of intersecting concavities ("hollow diamonds") like the faceting of stems were popular motives. In this way the cutting gave a heightened play of reflections, but did not greatly diminish transpar-ency. Candlesticks and tapersticks, which in this period naturally tended to become lighter, were often richly decorated with cutting. "Diamond-cut scalloped candlesticks" were advertised in 1742. To this period probably belong some of the well-known four-sided spirit-bottles, found in sets in rosewood travelling-cases. Many bottles of the kind are Bohemian glass made for the Dutch market; but "triangular bottles, stopped" in an advertisement of Thomas Betts (1756) suggests that some, at least, were made in England. Ten years later "Ladies' Dressing-boxes and Sweet-water bottles for the Ladies' Toilets" were advertised at Bath, as "from the stock-in-trade of a German who was the first that brought the art of Cutting and Engraving of Glass from Germany"; this is sometimes thought to have been Haedy, the Bohemian cutter already mentioned as employed by John Akerman as early as 1719. The greatest development of this English cut glass came later and will be further described presently.

Wheel-engraved decoration was obviously inspired by the German, but shows much less accomplishment. Fine and elaborate specimens are almost always suspected of being Dutch or German work, though perhaps done in England by immigrant craftsmen; armorial glasses of the kind are not un-common. But the native English style is seen in unpretentious borders of scrollwork and formal flowers. The first unmistakable advertisements of these date from 1735, and by 1742 "flowered glasses" were being commonly sold. The engraving is at its best in such simple motives as baskets of flowers, vine branches on wine glasses, hops and barley on glasses for ale, and apple-trees on cider glasses. But more ambitious pictorial subjects are not uncommon. Convivial scenes (inscribed "Keep it up") and hunting-subjects are often crude but charming. Landscapes with ruins, *chinoiseries* and naturalistic flowers, take up the subjects painted on the contemporary English porcelain. Seldom of great artistic merit are the engraved Jacobite glasses made for a couple of decades after the rising of 1745, with emblems and mottoes such as *"Fiat," "Radiat"* and *"Audentior Ibo,"* the rose with two buds, the sunflower, the butterflies and bees, and the stricken oak and sapling. Rough portraits of the Pretender are also found. On the rival Williamite

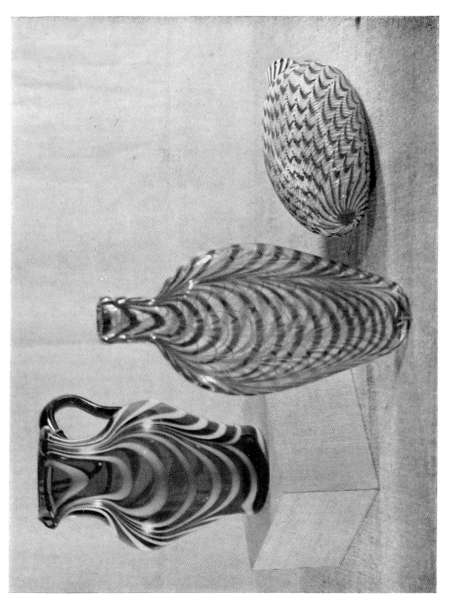

NAILSEA JUG AND FLASKS

Late eighteenth and first half of the nineteenth century

EARLY VICTORIAN GLASS FOUNTAIN WITH BIRDS

glasses are the orange-tree and equestrian portraits of William III with inscriptions such as *"The Immortal Memory."* Other glasses equally crude in engraving record the emotions of the Seven Years War (1756-63), when portraits of Frederick the Great and figures of Britannia were popular; other glasses of the time depict ships, with inscriptions such as *"Success to the British Fleet 1759,"* while *"Success to the Eagle Frigate"* on another glass refers to the raiding of French shipping by the Bristol privateers.

Perhaps the most attractively simple of all the engraved decoration is that on decanters; beautifully lettered "labels" indicate the destined contents. An advertisement of 1755 speaks of "new fashioned Decanters with inscriptions engraved on them, viz., Port, Claret, Mountain, etc., etc., decorated with Vine-leaves, Grapes, etc." Decanters began to be more commonly made in clear glass in this period, taking the place of the dark-green bottle-glass decanters to be described presently as belonging to a different strand in the English tradition. The globular shape of the rare earliest type was obviously suggested by the decanter bottles, and has a rim for tying down a cork. Later specimens with glass stoppers are commoner from about 1750 onwards. At first of club shape with prominent shoulder and spire stopper, they became more slender towards 1760 and were often provided with flat stoppers in the form of a vertical disc. Gently tapering forms remained in fashion until the last years of the 18th century.

Painting in enamel colours, though common in earlier Islamic and Continental (especially Venetian and German) glass, was apparently not attempted in England until the 18th century. But soon after 1750 two sorts of enamel-decoration were practised with great success. The most original work was done by a family named Beilby, of Newcastle-on-Tyne, in particular by William (b. 1740, d. 1819) and Mary (b. 1749, d. 1797), brother and sister of that Ralph Beilby, heraldic engraver, to whom Thomas Bewick was apprenticed in 1767. The earliest recorded Beilby glasses commemorate the birth of the Prince of Wales (afterwards George IV) and are presumed to date from 1762. They continue until about 1778, when William and Mary Beilby left Newcastle for Scotland. The signed glasses bear no initial and it is difficult to distinguish the work of brother and sister. The enamelling is exquisite in colour, a cool bluish white and a soft turquoise predominating. The vine-branches, rococo scrolls and trellis and waving foliage on the earlier tall knopped glasses were painted with an exceedingly free and sensitive touch; this is presumed to be early work of William Beilby. Perhaps the finest of all Beilby glasses is a bowl—the only one recorded—given to the Victoria and Albert Museum by the Rev. G. B. Riddell, in whose family it had been preserved. This is signed and dated 1765, and painted with arms, foliage and a group of trophies, and with rococo shell scrollwork and trellis pattern, all touched in with the utmost delicacy and feeling. Later work on air-twist and opaque-white-twist glasses was not always so good; the subjects included birds, rural pastimes, portraits of the Young Pretender, and electioneering

GROUP OF ENGRAVED GLASSES
Middle of the eighteenth century

appeals. The glasses used by the Beilby family give, incidentally, a fairly sure indication of the local Newcastle types.

The second important type of enamel-painting was on opaque white glass, and a conscious rivalry with porcelain is apparent; though the popularity of the material may have been due in part to its omission from the terms of the Excise Act. Its reputed association with Bristol is of long standing, though the final proof that it was made there is still lacking. There were makers of "enamel glass," as it was called, in London and elsewhere, as well as at Bristol, and examples in "Ravenscroft" forms have already been mentioned. But the supposed Bristol type of white glass is different from these and of a very distinct and beautifully "solid" milk-white colour. Not all of it was painted; plain vases and bottles exist with no more decoration than well-judged vertical ribbing. Many of the forms fairly closely follow Chinese porcelain models; trumpet-mouthed waisted beakers and oviform and baluster-shaped vases were made in sets or *garnitures*. Cornucopia-shaped flower-holders appear to copy Worcester porcelain. Candlesticks of admirably proportioned profiles, finely reeded, and four-sided tea-caddies were also characteristic. Much of the supposed Bristol painting is of delightful pseudo-Chinese figures, with lively diaper borders, in fresh colours among which red and

GROUP OF CUT GLASSES
Late eighteenth and early nineteenth centuries

green predominate. This work is by one easily recognisable hand, formerly
believed to be that of Michael Edkins, a Bristol artist who is recorded to have
painted "enamel glass" for Bristol manufacturers. But the argument for this
was based on the false identification of a Worcester teapot with this painting
as early Bristol porcelain. Painting by the same hand is also found on Staffordshire salt-glazed wares. Enamelling in the style of the Chinese *famille rose*
is associated with the *chinoiserie* subjects, again as on salt-glazed ware. Some
painting of naturalistic birds and tight bunches of flowers in porcelain style
by a different hand, on candlesticks and tea-caddies, was "authenticated" as
his work by Edkins' grandson. Some other sorts of opaque-white glass, as
well as much opal or "milk-and-water" glass were certainly made at Newcastle.

White glass was also used for *vinaigrettes* and scent-bottles, *étuis*, snuff-
boxes and the like, and these pretty toys are also customarily called Bristol.
But the painting on them—of pastoral figures, stars and diapers, flowers
and exotic birds—is distinct from that just described and often recalls that
on the enamelled metal boxes made in the Birmingham and South Staffordshire region, where the glass also may have been made. But London remained
the fashion-leading centre and it is probable that some, at least, of the

35

enamelled glass boxes, which were commonly cut all over with facets, were made there and decorated by London jewellers.

Blue glass (as well as purple and emerald green) was also used for the scent-bottles, and these again are called Bristol, though there is no proof of their making in that city, beyond a record that Michael Edkins enamelled "cans," beakers, and other objects (though not scent-bottles) of blue glass. That blue glass was, in fact, made at Bristol at a later period is shown by the mark of Isaac Jacobs on certain finger-bowls with gilt key-fret border of about 1795. His predecessor, Lazarus Jacobs, employed Michael Edkins between 1785 and 1787, and the gilt "labels" on decanters and other inscriptions on blue glass may well be Edkins' work. But much coloured glass was certainly made else-where, particularly in this period, when the stress on decoration brought by the Excise doubtless encouraged the makers to use it.

THE NEO-CLASSICAL PERIOD

IN the last quarter of the 18th century the rising vogue of cut glass and its increasing elaborateness called for substantial vessels, which owing to the Excise were costly to make. In 1777, 1781, and 1787, increased duties placed a still heavier burden on the English glass-industry, and there began an exodus of English glass-makers to Ireland, where there was no duty at all, which brought a somewhat questionable fame to Irish glass-making. At Waterford a new establishment was started in 1783 by George and William Penrose, merchants, with the help of a Stourbridge glass-maker named John Hill. At Dublin a London glass-cutter named Ayckbowm turned manu-facturer in 1799, while in 1771 a Bristol glass-man named Benjamin Edwards set up an establishment at Dromore, Co. Tyrone, moving it five years later to Belfast. Designers and workmen were very often English and it is almost impossible in most cases to separate the productions of the two countries.

The glass in the Anglo-Irish style, as it may be called, dating from about 1780 to 1825 (when an Excise Duty was first imposed on Irish glass), is chiefly remarkable for Classical shapes inclining to heaviness. This was the period of reaction against the frivolous rococo of the mid-18th century, with its fantastic departures from symmetry, in favour of a new Classical Roman severity. Deep cutting was favoured and commonly covered the whole sur-face of the piece. Parallel or intersecting deep grooves gave ridges and "raised diamonds" in high relief, and these were often further cut with crisscross or stars, giving the so-called "strawberry diamonds" or "hobnail" cutting. To these new resources were added the fluting and slicing and circular concavities of the previous period. Heavy decanters and urn-shaped wine-coolers and vases are typical; boat-shaped salad bowls on insignificant moulded feet are characteristic "Irish" productions. But the only fully authenticated Irish pieces are some rather trivial finger-bowls and decanters with indefinite moulded fluting at the base, bearing the names of Irish manufacturers in relief on the bottom.

Some imposing cut-glass chandeliers began to be made about 1760 or earlier. A specimen in the Victoria and Albert Museum which came from a Waterford church has diamond-cut curved branches proceeding from a stem made up of globes and balls of ogee outline; but this was evidently an importation from London, where a large trade in such things was done by one William Parker of Fleet Street. Some famous chandeliers in the Assembly Rooms at Bath were made by him and bear his name. In the Regency period a favourite form of chandelier was formed by chains of small pendant drops.

In contrast to the heavy "Irish" types stands the more peculiarly English glass of the last quarter of the 18th century. Slender forms in the Classical taste and shallow cutting accord well with the mounts in silver and Sheffield plate with which they are often associated. Excellent use was made of well-placed narrow horizontal bands of low-relief diamonds in combination with shallow fluting. Wine-glasses tended to have short stems with fluting or faceting about the base of the bowl, which was often of ogee form, and square cut or moulded feet.

VASE
Late eighteenth century

37

This phase of English glass-making corresponds to the period of Wedgwood's predominance in English pottery; forms show the same Classical influences, and engraving when used at all was largely confined to the same formal motives. In the early part of the 19th century, the fashion for cameo reliefs exploited by Wedgwood extended to glass, and in 1819, to be precise, a successful manufacturer named Apsley Pellatt actually patented a process for making "silvered" and "encrusted" cameos in glass; this he had apparently learnt from the French, who were doing similar work much earlier.

By the 19th century, the English cut glass had secured a great market on the Continent. The brilliance of its lead-metal gave it an advantage over the Bohemian; and in this form English glass has continued to be preferred. This has often been regretted, the prickly monstrosities of the 1840's (for example) being poor representatives of English taste.

BOTTLES AND JUGS
AND THE GLASS MADE FOR COUNTRY MARKETS

DURING the whole period of the Venetian fashions and of the development and triumph of English crystal, common green glass continued to be made in forms that unmistakably show a Roman ancestry.

DECANTER-BOTTLE
With medallion stamped : *T. Ridge* 1720

Though disregarded by collectors, this bottle-glass, with its natural colouring of brownish green, is in some ways more admirable than the refined and colourless product of Ravenscroft's researches. It is well seen in the wine-bottles of the type known as decanter-bottles, but perhaps better described as serving-bottles, in which wine was brought from the cask to the table. These were made from the middle of the 17th century to about 1750, in a well-established sequence of forms, leading up to the long-necked cylindrical modern wine-bottle

MODERN CARBOY
Green bottle-glass

39

suitable for storage in a bin. The practice of stamping a name and date on a pad of glass on the shoulder enables the evolution of shapes to be traced. The bottles were at first bulbous, with long neck and broad base with deep "kick"; from about 1680 to about 1735 the neck was shorter. Such bottles have continued to this day to be made for commercial and industrial purposes, their most distinguished direct descendants being the narrow-necked pear-shaped carboys, two or three feet high, used for the transport and storage of acids; these are objects of great beauty in form and material though disregarded by most people on account of their utilitarian purpose.

Bottle-glass was made at many places in London and the provinces, but an outstanding manufactory was at Nailsea, near Bristol, founded in 1788 by John Robert Lucas, a Bristol bottle-maker. Lucas sought to avoid paying some of the Excise Duty by making jugs and other vessels for domestic use in bottle-glass, which was taxed at a lower rate. These are usually of admirable form, their rich-greenish-brown material being diversified by irregular spotting and splashing of white; decoration was otherwise limited to a well-judged trailing of white threads round the neck and a crinkling of applied vertical bands. A second phase in the Nailsea production dates from the period of management of Robert Lucas Chance (1810–15), who in 1824 also took over a famous glass-house at Spon Lane, Birmingham, thus founding the still-existing firm of Chance Bros. In this period were made the typical Nailsea jugs, bowls and pocket-flasks decorated with loops of white or pink or blue or other contrasted colour. The new style is thought to have been due to French workers introduced by R. L. Chance. More sophisticated productions included glass walking-sticks and fantastically shaped tobacco-pipes for shop-windows, in the same pink-and-white style. The white and striped glass material was also used for the so-called rolling-pins, inscribed with mottoes such as "Be true to me," given by sailors to their wives.

The original Nailsea style was almost a branch of peasant art; and though inheriting the medieval and ultimately the Roman tradition, it was essentially English. The same native tradition was shared by other provincial glass-houses, in the Midlands, and especially in the North—in Yorkshire and at Newcastle and Sunderland. But it is usually impossible to assign a place of origin or even a date to the jugs, sugar-basins and simple vases made at these places, in green, blue, purple or opal-white glass. Some of them may date from the late 18th century, but most are later still, and the types continued to be made well into Victorian times. They were essentially country-market glasses, no doubt much sold at fairs and given as mementoes. All this simple coloured glass, which shows little refinement but excellent craftsmanship in shapes and handles, provided the models for several makes of early American glass. Much that is collected in America as Southern New Jersey, Pennsylvania, and Mid-Western work is scarcely distinguishable from this English provincial glass.

GLASS VASE AND BOWL DESIGNED BY KEITH MURRAY
Stevens & Williams, Limited, Brierly Hill, Stourbridge

LARGE GLASS VASE
James Powell & Sons, Limited, Whitefriars Glassworks, Wealdstone

VICTORIAN GLASS

THE Glass Excise came to an end in 1845 and the repeal was the signal for a great outburst of activity in glass-making, which had for some time previously been gathering force. The renowned Apsley Pellatt, already mentioned for his "encrusted cameos," was chiefly instrumental in a movement to revive past styles, while R. L. Chance of Birmingham was leader in a great advance in glass-technology. Colour in glass came into fashion again, inspired by the contemporary Bohemian renascence, but it was chiefly crude and harsh colour with a stress on strong reds and crimsons. All this activity found expression six years later in the Great Exhibition of 1851, which it should be remembered was held in the "Crystal Palace," then in Hyde Park, the first great building ever constructed chiefly of glass. The glassware exhibited was for the most part fantastically over-elaborate, showing an entirely mistaken belief in the value of applied ornament, and a misguided stress on size. Monstrous cut-glass fountains and chandeliers were made. Bohemian models were followed in "cased" or "flashed" glass, with coloured surface layer cut through to form a pattern. "Anglo-Venetian" glass, frosted or lavishly gilded, or of opal metal, was blown and manipulated into extravagant forms. So-called "Grecian," "Gothic," "Alhambra," and "Egyptian" work made a grotesque parody of former styles. Pressed glass, made in moulds after an American invention, figured largely at the Exhibition, and was used (as it still largely is) as a cheap means of roughly reproducing the appearance of cut glass.

Early Victorian glass, however, makes an appeal to one side of modern taste by its frequently amusing sentimentality; it is found to be so much old-fashioned nonsense, with period charm. Glass is of course a material that lends itself to fanciful play, and toys of many kinds may be fashioned from it. In the 18th century, we find glass swords being made, to be carried in processions, glass walking-sticks, practicable trumpets, and later on, exceedingly intricate models of ships. The fountain with long-tailed birds, here figured in colours, is a fitting companion to the wax fruits and stuffed owls similarly enclosed under domed glass shades in the early Victorian period. Its colour suggests that it too was made at Nailsea. The wonders of *millefiori* had been preached by Apsley Pellatt, and the Roman technique was now put to astonishing use in the making of paperweights in which the most prodigious "flowers" are seen growing at the bottom of a convex pool of clear glass.

After the orgy of the Exhibition, glass-making in common with other industrial arts set about to reform its ways, seeking with the help of the newly founded museums to achieve greater correctness in its imitation of past styles. Gothic now began to give place to Renaissance as the favourite style. In mid-Victorian times the Stourbridge School of Art helped the Stourbridge manufacturers to produce some faithful imitations of Roman cameo-glass, not without awareness of Chinese snuff-bottles. George and Thomas Woodall were noteworthy designers of this, and John Northwood is remembered for a reproduction of the most famous of all Roman cameo-glasses—the "Portland Vase." Painting on glass strove after a naturalism borrowed from porcelain, and particularly from Sèvres, and was much counterfeited in transfer-printing done by the newly invented process of colour-lithography. Towards 1875 a new influence came from Japan, then newly opened to Western trade; the asymmetrical foliate designs and diapers thus inspired eventually brought the style known as the *Art Nouveau*, at the end of the century. All the while cut glass in the Anglo-Irish styles, and pressed glass imitating it, continued to be made for both the English and the foreign markets, its "water-white" brilliance being still greatly admired. But until recent times no attempt was made to give it fresh treatment.

MODERN ENGLISH GLASS

SOON after the Exhibition, voices began to be raised in protest against the dishonesty of much of the "applied art" then fashionable, with its mechanically reproduced imitation of handwork, and its disregard of fitness for use. Ruskin with his theories and the practical sense of William Morris alike rose in protest, and in 1859 a landmark was reached when Morris commissioned Philip Webb to design for his use at the Red House, Bexley, some tumblers and wine-glasses, which were made for him by James Powell and Sons at the Whitefriars Glass-house in London. Fifteen years later, the same firm made other glasses for Morris to the design of another architect, T. G. (afterwards Sir Thomas) Jackson. From this time onwards the Whitefriars firm, under the direction of Harry J. Powell, began to recover the older and better tradition which prevailed in England before the fashion for extravagant cutting had obscured it. Not only finely manipulated glass in the English and Venetian manners, with trailed and tooled decoration, but austerely designed cut glass, simply faceted or fluted, was made at Whitefriars. In more recent times, the same firm (which in 1922 moved its premises to Wealdstone in Middlesex) has made much glass of fine quality to the design of Barnaby Powell, Tom Hill, James Hogan and others, depending for its appeal chiefly on skilful workmanship. No other modern glass surpasses Whitefriars in its exploitation, by subtle waving of surface and variation in thickness, of that interior play of light which is so essential a part of the beauty of glass; and no other firm has such lovely colour at command, in clear jewel-like blues and greens, amber and amethyst.

The cutting of glass, in spite of the bad example of the 19th century, may indeed be a veritable enhancement if used with imagination and restraint; and some of the Stourbridge firms have lately broken away from their "traditional" prickly extravagance so far as to employ independent designers of original talent. The most successful of these was the architect Keith

VASE DESIGNED BY CLYNE FARQUHARSON
John Walsh Walsh, Limited, Birmingham

Murray, who designed for Messrs. Stevens and Williams of Brierley Hill, Stourbridge, a range of plain and decorated vases, and some table wares, showing a profound appreciation of the qualities of the material, especially when cut. This Brierley Hill glass is chiefly a crystal of ice-like purity, though some rare dusky greens are also of unique quality. The light-dispersing character of English lead-glass, with its mysterious play of reflections, has probably never been better revealed than in Keith Murray's great vases and bowls with their austere faceting and grooving and slicing in half-moons. His designs for engraving might seem to challenge comparison to their disadvantage with the super-subtle contemporary Swedish work, but the strength and directness of their firmly stylised plant-forms—the "Cactus," "Thistledown" and others—make them in fact quite distinct. Other gifted designers, such as Graham Sutherland and Eric Ravilious for Stuart's, and Clyne Farquharson for John Walsh Walsh Ltd., of Birmingham, have done fine work occasionally, but none has shown quite the same mastery and understanding as Keith Murray during his short spell with the Brierley Hill firm.

But all such work as that just described, whether freely blown and wrought by a craftsman or ground down to an architect's paper plan, must at the present day rank as luxury art, aside from the main stream of development of glass-manufacture in England, where the machine has inevitably come to stay. However much we may crave it, hand-made glass is economically unreal, serving a luxury market and satisfying a self-conscious and sophisticated taste. In an age of mass-production and high wages handicraft is an anachronism, incapable of providing useful wares in such quantity as would make them available for all. However much we may regret the loss its coming

DECANTER AND GLASSES
James Powell & Sons, Limited, Whitefriars Glassworks

DECANTER AND GLASSES
Thomas Webb & Corbett, Limited, Stourbridge

implies we must recognise the machine as a potentially beneficent force in human society. Its association with a predatory commercialism is not necessary or inevitable, and in responsible hands it could bring amenities of many kinds into the lives of men and women at large. Already, in glass-manufacture, articles mass-produced by pressing are available at extremely low prices and only require the indispensable contribution of a designer of authentic talent to become works of art of a new order. Table-wares, containers for liquid merchandise, and a hundred articles of daily use are now made of glass largely by mechanical processes, and the principles that should govern their manufacture may well be regarded as more important at the present day than the merely decorative art of hand-made glass.

Many mass-produced vessels, undecorated and made for industrial, laboratory, and commercial uses, make no claim to be works of art but achieve that status largely through the unconscious artistry or sense of line and form of the engineer-designers responsible for them. And though few forms are

45

BOWL DESIGNED BY BARNABY POWELL
James Powell & Sons, Limited, Whitefriars Glassworks

absolutely determined by function there always seems to be a closer approach to what is felt to be the form dictated by the requirements of use. This is a matter of "period" taste common to handwork and machine-work alike.

Now the distinction between handwork and the art of the machine lies chiefly in the fact that the latter must lack the organic ("freehand") irregularity of the other. This is due to the nature of machine tools, which differ from the implements of the craftsman in that form is imparted to them with (as the word implies) mechanical regularity and perfection. The craftsman's design is worked out in the making, while machine work is comparable rather with the art of architecture, in which a studio-drawn design is carried out impersonally and the object may be multiplied endlessly without deviation. Thus in the mechanised making in glass of bottles and drinking-glasses, ovenware, storage-jars and jam-pots, flasks and carboys, scent-bottles and other articles for the toilet-table, preference should be given to novel plain but well-proportioned and harmonious forms, with no decoration save slight relief frankly produced by the mould, together with such simple adjuncts to form as faceting, fluting and reeding, contrasts of texture, and the "waving" of surface produced by an indefinite faceting softened in the furnace. Colour too is all-important, but need not always be bright colour. Smoky tones and greenish tinges may have an equal charm, and here modern chemistry may offer much valuable help.

In this essentially modern art English firms such as the great house of Chance Bros. and the vast undertaking known as the United Glass-Bottle Manufacturers have had a rare opportunity which they have not failed to take. The admirable American-designed "Pyrex" oven-ware has its English rival in "Phoenix," while the English perfume-bottles have shown themselves fully equal in attractiveness to the best work of the French glass-houses in a department formerly regarded as exclusively theirs.

Modern English glass-technology, in which a leading place is taken by the great College at Sheffield, has also found many new uses for the material, uses which lie outside the scope of this book but call for a word in conclusion. In architecture above all glass has been more and more employed in recent times as a covering for walls and ceilings, either plain white or in opaque colours or black, or in the form of large sheets of polished plate with engraved, etched or sandblasted decoration on a scale never attempted before. Outdoing the builders of the Crystal Palace, which had a framework of iron, our glass-architects have constructed whole walls entirely of glass-bricks, opening up a range of new possibilities. In this the great firm of Pilkington Bros. of St. Helen's have been pioneers.

Yet such uses must always rank below the making of glass vessels. In these alone is the wonder of glass fully revealed, with its translucency and luminous colour, its crystalline brilliance and the soft mysterious play of light within its substance. For this beauty of material no glass has ever surpassed the English.

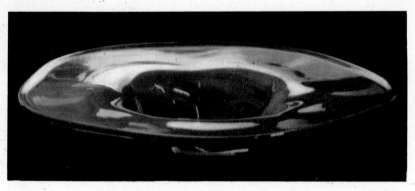

DISH DESIGNED AND MADE BY TOM HILL
James Powell & Sons, Limited, Whitefriars Glassworks

SHORT BIBLIOGRAPHY

Apsley Pellatt, *Curiosities of Glass-making*. London, 1849.—Albert Hartshorne, *Old English Glasses*. London and New York, 1897.—Harry J. Powell, *Glass-making in England*. Cambridge, 1923.—Francis Buckley, *Old English Glass*. London, 1925.—W. A. Thorpe, *A History of English and Irish Glass*. London, 1929.—W. A. Thorpe, *English Glass*. London, 1935.—Raymond McGrath and A. C. Frost, *Glass in Architecture and Decoration*. London, 1937. —Victoria and Albert Museum (W. B. Honey), *Glass: A Handbook for the study of Glass Vessels of all Countries and Periods, and a Guide to the Museum Collection*. London, 1946

OVEN-GLASS CASSEROLE
Phoenix Glassware Company, Birmingham